FOUR
BASICS OF
HEARING
GOD'S
VOICE

Andrew Wommack

Unless otherwise indicated, all Scripture quotations are taken from the King James Version® of the Bible. Copyright © by the British Crown. Public domain.

Scripture quotations marked NKJV are taken from the New King James Version®. Copyright © 1982 by Thomas Nelson. Used by permission. All rights reserved.

All emphasis within Scripture quotations is the author's own.

Published in partnership between Andrew Wommack Ministries and Harrison House Publishers.

Woodland Park, CO 80863 – Shippensburg, PA 17257

ISBN 13 TP: 978-1-59548-573-1

For Worldwide Distribution, Printed in the USA

1 2 3 4 5 6 / 26 25 24 23

CONTENTS

INTRODUCTION

D id you know that God is always speaking? If you didn't know that, you're probably not hearing Him speak to you very well. It's one of the reasons you're facing some of the challenges in life. But if you could hear God clearly, it would not only get you out of problems, but it would help you avoid them altogether! Honestly, I don't know how anyone makes it without hearing God's voice. It is an absolute essential! And yet, the majority of Christians are content to go through life not even knowing that He is speaking to them, let alone how. If that's you, I have some good news that will really help you.

It might not surprise you to hear that there is more than one way God can speak to you. However, you might not know the basics of how to hear His voice. I tell you, there are specific ways that He communicates; and if you would learn them, you will be able to discern whether what you're hearing is God, if it's the devil, or if it's just your own heart and desires. I want to share with you four basic ways that God speaks. These have not only helped me but countless others who've heard me share these truths.

I say this in love, but if your life just seems like it's totally out of whack—whether it be in your body, your finances, your emotions, or in your marriage—I can guarantee you, it's because you have been making decisions independent of hearing God. Now, you don't have to stay there. You're just one word away from God from seeing that whole situation turned around. But you need to learn the basics of what I will be sharing in this booklet. It will increase your confidence in your relationship with God, and you will have a totally different life!

CHAPTER 1

YOUR CONSCIENCE

The most fundamental way that you can hear from God and be led by Him is with your conscience. It is an intuitive knowledge in your heart of right and wrong. When God made Adam and Eve, He didn't create them with a conscience. But when they disobeyed Him by eating of the Tree of the Knowledge of Good and Evil, they realized they were naked and started experiencing fear over their sin (Gen. 3:7–10). That was the conscience becoming active, and every human being after them would also have a conscience. In the book of Romans, Paul wrote about the people who don't even know the Lord:

> *Which shew the work of the law written in their hearts, their conscience also bearing witness, and* their *thoughts the mean while accusing or else excusing one another.*

> Romans 2:15

Your conscience will either accuse you or excuse you, and it functions automatically. This wasn't part of God's original plan, but after sin entered in, the conscience became a necessary way of discerning His voice.

Nevertheless, the conscience is not infallible. Our conscience is influenced by what we believe. Wrong thinking can pervert our conscience so it condemns us over things that are not wrong, just as right thinking can actually strengthen the assurance coming from our conscience. As a matter of fact, 1 John 3:18–19 says you have to assure your heart before God. That means you can get to the place where your conscience actually gives you confidence:

> *For if our heart condemn us, God is greater than our heart, and knoweth all things. Beloved, if our heart condemn us not,* then *have we confidence toward God.*
>
> 1 John 3:20–21

If you can learn to assure your heart, then your conscience will give you confidence. The apostle Paul said two different times that he strived constantly to have a conscience without offense (Acts 23:1 and 24:16). That doesn't mean he was sinless or that he ignored his conscience. It just means he practiced, as a lifestyle, to keep his conscience clear. He put effort into it. This is part of how you assure your heart.

Condemnation vs. Conviction

You are going to fall short. You're going to do something that you know is wrong, or you're not going to do something that you know you should have done. What do you do with your conscience then? The Bible says that the blood of Christ will purge your conscience from dead works to serve the living God (Heb. 9:14). When you commit sin, whether by commission or omission, you don't need to sit there and wallow in misery. You need to be quick to stand on the blood of Jesus to receive forgiveness and cleansing (1 John 1:9). No one is perfect, so you need to learn to be strong in the grace that is in the Lord Jesus (2 Tim. 2:1).

> **If you can learn to assure your heart, then your conscience will give you confidence.**

Satan is the accuser of the brethren (Rev. 12:10). He'll try to use your conscience to condemn you, but you overcome him by the blood of the Lamb and by the word of your testimony (Rev. 12:11). If you strive to keep a good conscience, you will stop him from having opportunity against you and stop his condemnation. This is a major part of learning to discern God's voice.

Conviction is from the Lord, whereas condemnation is from the devil (John 16:7–11). God will use conviction to prick your conscience when you rebel against Him. He will not just affirm everything in your life. But conviction will never come to hurt you or to cause fear. God will only use it to draw you back to Himself. This is a normal function of the conscience.

DO THE GOOD YOU KNOW TO DO

While the conscience is not a totally reliable guide for hearing the voice of the Lord, it would be to your own detriment to just ignore or violate it. Every time you did, you would be putting a layer of insensitivity between you and God and making it that much harder to hear from Him. Eventually, you could get to the place where you actually sear your conscience (1 Tim. 4:2).

If you get a cut that needs stitches but are unable to get it treated, you can take a hot iron to the wound to cauterize it. The nerve endings would be killed so you wouldn't have any feeling there. This is what 1 Timothy 4:2 is speaking of happening to your conscience—the foundational way God speaks to you. If you sever your conscience from functioning, you could be given over to a reprobate mind (Rom. 1:28). That is a person who has totally destroyed any sense of right and wrong within them. This describes what the conscience does. Once that happens and God stops drawing them, there is no return. They can't be saved.

You need to get to where you do what you know is right in your heart. If you want to hear the voice of God, it all starts here. You can't skip over this. Make a decision that you are not going to live a life of intentionally doing wrong.

James 4:17 says,

Therefore to him that knoweth to do good, and doeth it not, to him it is sin.

Yes, God loves you whether you sin or whether you don't. He's not mad at you. But you are not going to hear His voice very well if you go against what you know in your heart. If you aren't listening to your conscience and you're into willful sin, why should God show you anything else? It says in Luke 12:48b, *"Unto whomsoever much is given, of him shall be much required."* If God were to speak to you in ways beyond the conscience, that'd just make you more accountable. Out of His love for you, He won't do that. You have to first be responsible with what you've been given before God speaks to you in other ways (Luke 16:10). Choose today not to ignore or violate your conscience!

CHAPTER 2

HIS WORD

The next way God speaks to you is through His Word. You can hear things beyond the Word of God, but nothing will ever contradict or supersede it. This is the plumbline by which you measure everything you say God is speaking to you. That's why you need to:

> *Study to shew thyself approved unto God, a workman that needeth not to be ashamed, rightly dividing the word of truth.*
>
> 2 Timothy 2:15

If something doesn't match up with the Word of God, don't receive it.

How do you discern whether what you think you are hearing from God is actually His voice? Hebrews 4:12, *NKJV* says,

For the word of God is living and powerful, and sharper than any two-edged sword, piercing even to the division of soul and spirit, and of joints and marrow, and is a discerner of the thoughts and intents of the heart.

When you think God may be speaking to you, the Word of God will discern whether it's really from Him or not.

TRANSFORMED AND RENEWED

My personal testimony directly speaks to this. You have probably heard about my supernatural encounter with the Lord on March 23, 1968. But the eighteen months prior to that event is what led to God revealing His will for my life.

When I was getting ready to graduate from high school, I had to decide what I was going to do next. So, I really started seeking the Lord. I knew somewhere in the Bible was my answer, so I got serious about reading the Word. For months, all I did was read through Scripture. I would stay up until two or three o'clock in the morning. I didn't want to sleep; I wanted to know God's will for my life! That's how hungry I was. One day, when I was reading the Word, I came across a scripture in Romans, chapter 12:

I beseech you therefore, brethren, by the mercies of God, that ye present your bodies a living sacrifice, holy, acceptable unto God, which is *your reasonable service. And be not conformed to this world: but be ye transformed by the renewing of your mind, that ye may prove what* is *that good, and acceptable, and perfect, will of God.*

Romans 12:1–2

When I read that, it was like God put a spotlight on it. That's what I'd been after! For the next four months, from December 1967 until March 1968, all I did was meditate on Romans 12:1 and 2, praying, "What does it mean to be a living sacrifice? What does it mean to be transformed by the renewing of my mind?" I knew that if I could figure that out, then I would know the good, the acceptable, and the perfect will of God.

At this time, I was getting together with my friends on Saturday nights for a prayer meeting. At midnight on March 23, God showed up. I didn't physically see anything, and I didn't audibly hear anything, but I knew I was in the presence of the Lord. The glory of God was there!

Up until this time, I had become a religious Pharisee. I'd been born again for ten years, and I was under the deception that I had to live holy for God to love me, accept me, and move in my life. I was living holier than anybody I knew and had become self-righteous. But when God showed up and I saw His glory and holiness, all of my righteousness looked like filthy rags (Is. 64:6). I honestly thought that God was going to kill me that night. However, before He would, I was going to confess everything I had ever done and everything I would ever do. I spent an hour and a half turning myself inside out repenting.

Then, instead of God killing me, I experienced a supernatural flow of God's love, and I was caught up into the presence of God that lasted for four and a half months! It was such a powerful encounter that I knew I was going to spend the rest of my life trying to share what God had revealed to me. This is how I began to prove God's perfect will for my life. It all started through reading and meditating on the Word of God. This is how God still speaks to me today.

I'm sure you would like to have God speak to you. (You wouldn't be reading this booklet otherwise.) But would you spend eighteen months just reading the Word, even if you're sleepy? It's not a formula, but very few people are that hungry. Then they wonder why they don't hear God. You've got to have a commitment to the Word of God.

God's Word Is Perfect

There are a lot of Christians who don't even believe that the Bible is infallible. They believe that it contains His Word but that it can't be trusted completely. However, outside of Jesus coming and then leaving the Holy Spirit for us, the Bible is the most important way for you to hear the voice of God.

Psalm 19:7 says,

The law of the LORD is perfect, converting the soul: the testimony of the LORD is sure, making wise the simple.

The Bible is not just good, and it's doesn't just contain the Word of God. It is perfect, and it is the Word of God. It will teach you everything you need to know. As a matter of fact, the Greek word used for the phrase *inspiration of God*[1] in the following passage literally means the Word is God-breathed:

> **The Bible is the most important way for you to hear the voice of God.**

All scripture is given by inspiration of God, and is profitable for doctrine, for reproof, for correction, for

---

[1] Vine's Expository Dictionary of New Testament Words, s.v. "Inspiration of God," accessed February 28, 2023, https://www.blueletterbible.org/search/Dictionary/viewTopic.cfm?topic=VT0001509.

instruction in righteousness: That the man of God may be perfect, throughly furnished unto all good works.

2 Timothy 3:16–17

The apostle Peter, in an effort to show that the Word of God wasn't just man's opinion, wrote,

For he received from God the Father honour and glory, when there came such a voice to him from the excellent glory, This is my beloved Son, in whom I am well pleased. And this voice which came from heaven we heard, when we were with him in the holy mount. We have also a more sure word of prophecy; whereunto ye do well that ye take heed, as unto a light that shineth in a dark place, until the day dawn, and the day star arise in your hearts.

2 Peter 1:17–18

On the Mountain of Transfiguration, Peter had seen the glory of God come and overshadow him. He even heard the audible voice of God. And yet, he said, *"We have also a more sure word of prophecy"* (2 Pet. 1:19a). What can be more sure than hearing God's voice or seeing a visible manifestation of His glory? He went on to write,

Knowing this first, that no prophecy of the scripture is of any private interpretation. For the prophecy came

not in old time by the will of man: but holy men of God spake as they were *moved by the Holy Ghost.*

2 Peter 1:20–21

The word *moved*, if you look it up in *Vine's Expository Dictionary of Old and New Testament Words*, means that the writers of the Bible were moved along by the Holy Spirit. What they wrote was born by the Spirit. The words of Scripture aren't the opinions of fallible man. No, they're inspired. This is one of the ways God has chosen to communicate to us. It is critical to believe this if we're going to hear His voice.

Speaking about the Israelites who had come out of the land of Egypt and were promised a land flowing with milk and honey, Hebrews 4:2 says,

The word preached did not profit them, not being mixed with faith in them that heard it.

I want to encourage you to have faith that God will speak to you through His Word. Then it will benefit and help you.

MEDITATE ON THE WORD

It takes more than just reading the Word to hear from God. You have to meditate in it daily. This is a prerequisite for you to be prosperous and to have good success:

This book of the law shall not depart out of thy mouth; but thou shalt meditate therein day and night, that thou mayest observe to do according to all that is written therein: for then thou shalt make thy way prosperous, and then thou shalt have good success.

Joshua 1:8

This is powerful! If you aren't experiencing either good or success, it's because you've departed from meditating on the precepts of the Word of God. This is how God speaks to you. Why in the world would God speak to you any other way if you don't honor what He said in His Word?

People have died to give us the Bible, and most of us ignore it at best. At worst, we don't even believe it. If we do believe it, we don't spend much time in it. And if that's the case, we don't have to look any farther than this as to why God isn't speaking to us.

To say it another way, if we aren't letting the Word of God influence our thinking, then we're letting this world's system influence our thinking. We have a choice whether to be conformed to this world or to be transformed by the renewing of our minds. Let God be true and every man a liar (Rom. 3:4). His Word has to be absolute truth and the final authority in our lives.

God's Word Is a Seed

Over in 1 Peter 1:23, the Word is referred to as a seed.

Being born again, not of corruptible seed, but of incorruptible, by the word of God, which liveth and abideth for ever.

You have to take this seed and plant it in the soil of your heart (Mark 4:3–32). And if you do that, the seed becomes activated and begins to produce. You've got everything in Christ that you'll ever need, but the seed has to be sown. Then it needs to be watered and cultivated. If you'll cooperate with this process, the Word will be life unto you and health to all of your flesh (Prov. 4:20–22).

> **If we aren't letting the Word of God influence our thinking, then we're letting this world's system influence our thinking.**

You may agree with what I've said in this chapter, but you may not be living it right now. You've let other things choke the Word of God: the cares of this life, the deceitfulness of riches, and the lust other things (Mark 4:19). You've got to get to a place that you not only say you believe it, but you do it. Faith without works is dead (James 2:20). I guarantee that if you will meditate in the Word of God day and night, you will make your way prosperous, and you will have good success. This applies to hearing God's voice in every area of your life.

I believe that God is leading you to make a commitment to the Word of God right now. Make it a priority in your life that you'll not go another day without letting it dominate and impact you. God will speak to you!

CHAPTER 3

YOUR SPIRIT

When you are born again, you are one spirit with the Lord (1 Cor. 6:17). This is a reality in the spiritual realm. Most Christians are not conscious of what's true in the spirit. They identify more with who they are according to the flesh than who they are in Christ. But who you are in the spirit is the real you.

You don't have to live by this physical, natural realm, looking for God to speak to you through your circumstances or by some kind of outward sign. There's a better way. You can walk by faith and not by sight (2 Cor. 5:7) and let God speak to you Spirit to spirit! Instead of God's voice coming from the outside in, through an external sign, or in third person, it'll be from the inside out, in first person. You'll just know what God is saying in your spirit.

Now, right off the bat, you might be asking, "How do I know if what I'm hearing is not just my mind or my flesh?"

Again, the Word of God discerns between soul and spirit and the thoughts and intents of the heart (Heb. 4:12). With the Word of God, you can know whether what you're hearing is the flesh part of you or whether it is the born-again part of you. That's why, as I shared in the last chapter, it is so important that you know the Word. You're at a deficit in being able to discern His voice if you don't. Satan will use that disadvantage against you, and you'll be deceived.

Now, it is possible to put so much emphasis on the Bible that you don't follow the Spirit. But you can be out of balance either way. There was a woman who came to me and said she had a dream where I was on the beaches of Normandy in World War II. All around me were land mines. She said, "Which would you rather have: a map that told you where every mine was or a voice behind you telling you where to step?" She was trying to illustrate that it was better to have the voice and be led by the Spirit than by the Bible. But when she said that, I thought, *Neither one of them are enough on their own. How would you know whether you're hearing the voice correctly or that the voice can be trusted? Then, how do you know that you're reading the map right?* However, if you put the voice together with the map, one can confirm the other. It takes the Word and the Spirit! You've got to have both.

PEACE LIKE AN UMPIRE

In your spirit, you know all things (1 John 2:20). Most people say, "Well, that's not true. I can't even find my glasses, and they're on top of my head!" With your mind, you don't know all things, but in your spirit, you do know all things. I'm pretty sure you have had a decision to make and you made the logical choice, but it didn't feel right. When things didn't work out, you said, "I knew I shouldn't have done that." That was your born-again spirit being led by God. Your spirit knew exactly what to do, but you followed your head instead of being led by peace. Over in Colossians, chapter 3, Paul wrote,

And let the peace of God rule in your hearts.

Colossians 3:15a

The word for *rule* means that peace is to be like an umpire in your heart. It's supposed to make the call whether something is of God or not. It won't be based on your circumstances. It'll be an inner knowing. But you will have to seek God in order to discern it.

> With your mind, you don't know all things, but in your spirit, you do know all things.

Isaiah 26:3 says that the Lord will *"keep* him *in perfect peace,* whose *mind* is *stayed on [Him]: because he trusteth in [Him]."* If you don't have peace in any direction, it's because your mind is not stayed on God. You're stayed on the problem. If you're sitting there watching filth on television, the carnal mind is enmity against God (Rom. 8:7). You aren't going to have peace.

Nevertheless, having a peace about something does not mean you'll be void of problems. It won't be based on your circumstances. There is a peace that passes understanding (Phil. 4:7). Of the fruit of the Spirit (Gal. 5:22–23), I believe it is the easiest to discern.

This is what I would encourage you to do if you're new to hearing the voice of the Lord and you're struggling to discern peace: You either need to have a mentor to give you counsel and wisdom, or if you don't have a mentor, you can really slowly head in the direction that you feel the most peace. That peace will either increase, or if you're moving in the wrong direction, there will be a lack of peace. The spirit within you will not bear witness with a wrong decision.

I can tell you that the times when I've really messed up, it's been because I didn't let peace rule in my heart. I just did what was the wisest thing to do, or I caved to the pressure of circumstances. But anytime I've followed the peace of God in my heart, it has never failed me.

In your heart, you may have a holy dissatisfaction about your life right now. It's God taking away peace. He's making you uncomfortable because He's trying to get you out of the nest so you can do something different. He doesn't want you to be satisfied where you are. You need to follow the peace of God, and start making some changes.

When God Is Your Delight . . .

Another way God speaks through your spirit is through your own desires. Now, your brain might have just gone tilt, and there is a prerequisite to this, but it's true. In Psalm 37:4, it says,

> *Delight thyself also in the LORD; and he shall give thee the desires of thine heart.*

This is not saying that God is just going to give you anything you want. But if you are truly delighting in God, if you will put Him first place, then He will put His desires in your heart. In fact, He will change your desires. They will become His desires. I'm sure you have experienced this before. When you were born again, you no longer wanted to be a drunk, a doper, an adulterer, or whatever you were. God had changed your heart. The same principle still applies today: When you start delighting yourself in the Lord, He will bring to pass the desires of your heart.

You know, I was raised in the Baptist Church and was literally taught that if I wanted to know God's will, I just needed to take what I want and do the exact opposite. But that would only be good instruction for a totally carnal Christian! If you're delighting in God, you can actually reach a place where He puts His desires in your heart. Then whatever you do will be His will!

Now, you may struggle at first with what I'm about to say but because my spirit is in union with God and I delight in Him, I do whatever I want to do. I go where I want to go. People ask me, "Would you please pray about this?" and I say, "Well, I don't have to pray about this. I just do what I want to do." Now, you might have just choked on that, thinking, *That's terrible!* But I tell you, back in March 1968, I ran up a white flag and gave myself to God. I haven't lived it perfectly. However, for over half a century, my desire has been to live for God with everything I'm worth. I believe this is consistent with everything I read in the Word and what I've shared with you so far. When you put the Spirit with the map and they harmonize, I take that as being God. I start moving in that direction, and it comes to pass.

The Lord told me to quit limiting Him by my small thinking, through Psalm 78:41. He used Scripture to speak to me, which I'll talk more on in the next chapter. But I don't want to do anything just for myself. I am not building a legacy for me. My vision is to know God and to be in relationship with Him. That's really the only thing I care about. If God told me, "I want you to move to Africa and minister to people in a grass hut," I could do it. It wouldn't bother me. I would turn everything over to somebody else. (I might be going by myself—I'm not sure my wife Jamie would live in a grass hut!) But kidding aside, I'm not out to get God to fulfill my vision. I'm just delighting myself in the Lord and doing what He gives me a desire to do.

This has been my experience and what has worked for me. It'll work for you too. If you will delight in God, He will give you the desires of your heart. You can do what you want to do.

CHAPTER 4

THE HOLY SPIRIT

The final way I want to share with you about how to hear God's voice is through the power of the Holy Spirit. I could talk about the gift of prophecy, the word of wisdom, or the word of knowledge, but I don't have the space here to get into all of the gifts of the Spirit. I really want to focus on 1 Corinthians 2, where the apostle Paul wrote,

> And my speech and my preaching was not with enticing words of man's wisdom, but in demonstration of the Spirit and of power: That your faith should not stand in the wisdom of men, but in the power of God.
>
> 1 Corinthians 2:4–5

Paul said it wasn't his charisma or his oratorical abilities that allowed him to make such an impact. He came in the power of the Holy Spirit so that the faith of the believers

27

at Corinth would not be in the wisdom of man but in the power of God. Likewise, you need more than human ability to accomplish God's will for your life. It's going to take power beyond what you're able to produce.

The next couple of verses say,

> *Howbeit we speak wisdom among them that are perfect: yet not the wisdom of this world, nor of the princes of this world, that come to nought: But we speak the wisdom of God in a mystery,* even *the hidden* wisdom, *which God ordained before the world unto our glory.*

1 Corinthians 2:6–7

You need revelation, which only comes from the Holy Spirit. You don't need to figure things out with just your brain. You need to go beyond your thinking and let the Holy Spirit reveal the wisdom of God to you. It's wisdom that comes by revelation, not by education.

The Holy Spirit will lead you into all truth and even show you things to come (John 16:13). How beneficial would it be for God to show you that a train wreck is up ahead or that the plane you're getting ready to board will go down? Not only will the Holy Spirit tell you about the future, but He will also bring to your remembrance what Jesus said (John 14:26).

You need to depend upon Him to supernaturally quicken revelation to you.

Going back to 1 Corinthians 2, Paul wrote,

Eye hath not seen, nor ear heard, neither have entered into the heart of man, the things which God hath prepared for them that love him (v. 9).

You will hear people say, "Well, we just can't understand the things of God. Further along we'll know all about it, further along we'll understand why. Cheer up, my brethren. Live in the sunshine. We'll all understand it more by and by." That's from an old song that was written about this verse, and religion has just embraced this understanding and relegated the Christian life to being powerless and void of revelation. But look at the next verse:

But God hath revealed them unto us by his Spirit: for the Spirit searcheth all things, yea, the deep things of God.

1 Corinthians 2:10

With our little peanut-sized brains, we can't understand the things of God, but with our hearts, with the Holy Spirit giving us revelation, we can understand! The things of God are spiritually discerned (1 Cor. 2:14).

The Baptism of the Holy Spirit

Specifically, if you want to hear the voice of God, if you want to be led by God, you are going to have to receive the baptism of the Holy Spirit, which includes speaking in tongues. Let me share some verses with you from 1 Corinthians 14:

> *For he that speaketh in an* unknown *tongue speaketh not unto men, but unto God: for no man understandeth* him; *howbeit in the spirit he speaketh mysteries.*

> 1 Corinthians 14:2

Did you know that speaking in tongues is not gibberish? You can't understand it with your mind, but it is language (Acts 2:4–11). Remember, 1 Corinthians 2:7 says, "*We speak the wisdom of God in a mystery,* even *the hidden* wisdom." When you speak in tongues, you are speaking the mysteries of God.

Now, speaking in tongues is not something you do just to prove that you've received the baptism of the Holy Spirit. The reason to speak in tongues is because of the benefits that it

> **If you want to hear the voice of God, if you want to be led by God, you are going to have to receive the baptism of the Holy Spirit.**

offers. For instance, one of the reasons speaking in tongues is so powerful is it makes no sense to your brain. I may have lost you there, but keep reading.

We have all been taught to approach things with logic. We don't want to look foolish. We want to be perceived as being intelligent. But when we're speaking in tongues, our minds don't know what we're saying. This bothers a carnal Christian because something is going on that their minds don't control or understand. Their minds will begin to wander, and ultimately, they will rebel at speaking in tongues. But one of the reasons speaking in tongues doesn't make sense to us is so we'll get beyond our minds and through faith, put our focus on the Lord and trust Him!

I can tell you from experience that praying in tongues makes me focus not on my problems and what's going on in the natural realm, but it makes me focus on God. I can't continue to pray in tongues if I'm sitting here thinking on the negative. I hope you're hearing what I'm saying. So many things of this world are competing for your attention.

It's like Peter walking on the water and being distracted by the wind and the waves. As long as his focus was on Jesus, he walked on the water. But when he took his eyes off of Jesus, he began to sink. When you get to looking at all of the negative things in this world, the negative things that you've done, or the negative things that are being done to you, you will be overcome. But if you pray in tongues, over a prolonged period of time, it forces you to focus on God, which will pay huge dividends in your life. This is just invaluable.

As a matter of fact, 1 Corinthians 14:4a says,

He that speaketh in an unknown *tongue edifieth himself.*

The word *edify* here means to build up, to promote spiritual growth. Over in Jude 20, it says,

But ye, beloved, building up yourselves on your most holy faith, praying in the Holy Ghost."

When you pray in tongues, you build yourself up on your most holy faith. It edifies you. Isaiah prophesied that speaking in tongues would be the rest with which God would cause the weary to rest (Is. 28:12). If you're baptized in the Holy Spirit and have the gift of speaking in tongues, there really isn't any excuse for you to be depressed, worried, or defeated. There may be reasons why you're that way, but there is no excuse. The good news is, you don't have to stay that way! Speaking in tongues will build you up, edify you, give you rest, and refresh you.

You've got what no Old Testament saint had available to them: Shadrach, Meshach, and Abednego didn't have the baptism of the Holy Spirit, and yet they were able to stand strong and escape death despite being thrown into a fiery furnace (Dan. 3:24–27). Daniel was able to be thrown into a den of lions and be delivered (Dan. 6:16–23). What you have is so much better that what they had. You just have to get what's in you out. Speaking in tongues is one of the ways you do it!

PRAY THAT YOU MAY INTERPRET

Did you know that the one whom God used to write half of the books of the New Testament--Paul—was not one of Jesus' twelve disciples? In fact, he was a man who previously hated Jesus. However, after he encountered Jesus on the road to Damascus and got his life turned around, he ended up knowing Jesus better than His twelve apostles! I believe that one of the reasons for this is he had such a hunger to know the Lord (Phil. 3:10). The Bible says that those who hunger and thirst for righteousness shall be filled (Matt. 5:6). But how does this knowledge come? Through revelation by the Holy Spirit.

Now, some people might say, "No, Paul was a disciple of Gamaliel, a doctor of the Law. He was an educated man!"

They would attribute Paul's revelation to his education. Well, that is true: Paul certainly had an advantage over others, according to the flesh, which he made clear in Philippians 3:4–7. Apostles Peter and John, meanwhile, were said to be unlearned and ignorant men (Acts 4:13). But that isn't where Paul said he got his revelation. He wrote in Galatians 1:11–12,

I certify you, brethren, that the gospel which was preached of me is not after man. For I neither received it of man, neither was I taught it, but by the revelation of Jesus Christ.

A few verses later, Paul went on to say,

But when it pleased God, who separated me from my mother's womb, and called me by his grace, To reveal his Son in me, that I might preach him among the heathen; immediately I conferred not with flesh and blood: Neither went I up to Jerusalem to them which were apostles before me; but I went into Arabia, and returned again unto Damascus.

Galatians 1:15–17

What was Paul doing in Arabia? He was being taught by the Holy Spirit the message of grace. In other words, even with all of his education, Paul still needed revelation of what we call the Gospel today.

Speaking of Paul's revelation, Peter wrote,

Even as our beloved brother Paul also according to the wisdom given unto him hath written unto you; As also in all his epistles, speaking in them of these things; in which are some things hard to be understood, which they that are unlearned and unstable wrest, as they do also the other scriptures, unto their own destruction.

2 Peter 3:15b–16

Peter equated what Paul wrote to Scripture—that more sure word of prophecy he spoke about in 2 Peter 1:19–21. He recognized that even though he lived with Jesus day and night for three and a half years, he struggled to understand the things that Paul knew. Amazing!

I believe that Paul provided insight into his life of how he received the revelation that he had. He taught the Corinthian believers,

Wherefore let him that speaketh in an unknown tongue pray that he may interpret.

1 Corinthians 14:13

Paul went on to write that when he prayed in tongues, it was his spirit praying (1 Cor. 14:14). In your spirit, you have the mind of Christ (1 Cor. 2:16). I referenced 1 John 2:20 in the last chapter that you have an unction from the Holy One, and you know all things. That's talking about your spirit—the part of you that prays in tongues—that knows all things. But the knowledge in your spirit doesn't do you any good until you get it out into your physical mind. That's why, when you pray in tongues, you need to also pray that you interpret. It's like sticking a bucket down into the well of your spirit and drawing out the hidden wisdom that you're speaking.

That doesn't mean that speaking in tongues and having an interpretation can supersede the Word of God. But if you would take the Word of God, pray in tongues, and ask for an interpretation, the Holy Spirit will give you supernatural revelation. This is how Paul received the revelation that he had! As a matter of fact, he spoke in tongues more than all the Corinthians (1 Cor. 14:18). You need to be praying in tongues a lot and then asking for an interpretation! I have done this thousands of times.

I also want to mention that Paul wasn't saying that he prayed more than all the Corinthians in a church service. He said that he would rather speak five words with his understanding than ten thousand words in an unknown tongue in church so that people could be edified (1 Cor. 14:19). He was saying that he prayed in tongues privately more than all of them. So, when you're by yourself, you can pray in tongues as long as you want; you don't always need to interpret.

GROANING IN THE SPIRIT

When you don't know how to pray, the Scripture talks about groaning in the Spirit, which is a step beyond praying in tongues:

Likewise the Spirit also helpeth our infirmities: for we know not what we should pray for as we ought: but the Spirit itself maketh intercession for us with groanings which cannot be uttered. And he that searcheth the hearts knoweth what is *the mind of the Spirit, because he maketh intercession for the saints according to* the will of *God.*

Romans 8:26–27

The Holy Spirit will take hold together with you and help you intercede. He doesn't intercede for you without your participation. If He did, you would be totally set free, healed, delivered, and prosperous in every area of your life. It's a partnership. When you operate in groaning in the Spirit, supernatural things will happen. For example, if you're praying for someone to be saved, and you don't know why they haven't responded, you can intercede with the Holy Spirit and see things accomplished. It's a powerful gift, and it's not limited to praying in tongues.

Before I conclude this chapter, I want to share with you three examples of how I've seen God use praying in tongues. As I've mentioned, so much of what God has accomplished in my life has been come through praying in tongues and then asking Him for an interpretation.

KNOWLEDGE AND WISDOM FOR PROVISION

Before we started our first building project in 2002, the Lord spoke to me that I had limited Him by my small thinking. So, I made the decision to change and start believing big. We took out a loan of $3.2 million for the purchase of a new building in Colorado Springs. But then it was going to cost another $3.2 million to renovate the new building. Until all that was done, we wouldn't be able to occupy the building. The lending institution told us that they wouldn't have loaned us the money for the purchase if we hadn't also qualified for the loan for the renovation. They said we'd have the construction money in two weeks. But nine months went by, and we still didn't receive the loan for the renovation. Every week or so, we'd meet with the lending people, and they would find out something else that we needed to do.

So, they kept kicking this can down the road. Keep in mind that because I had stopped limiting God, the ministry was exploding. It was beginning to look like we would have to turn people away from coming to our Bible college. That was just not acceptable. We needed this new building!

After the nine months, I remember meeting with the loan people again, and they said, "You know, it's been a year since we did an appraisal on the property. Things have changed so much that it would be good for us to obtain a new appraisal and start the whole process over again." When they said that, I thought, *No way!* I told them, "Let me pray about it." I needed to hear from God! I went home and went on a walk to pray. I said, "Father, I have to have a word from you about what we're doing with this building. I'm going to pray in tongues and pray for an interpretation because my spirit knows the answer. My spirit has an unction from the Holy One, and it knows all things. I need to get what's in my spirit out into my brain!"

Before I could walk very far, God reminded me of a prophecy I had received from Dave Duell two years before then. He had said that I was not going to have to take out a loan for the building, because I owned a bank. When he had said that, I thought, *What bank do I own?* He said, "Your partners are your bank. You can't build more than your partners can supply debt-free." For whatever reason, I had totally forgotten about that prophecy! But within one minute, God brought it to mind. Now, I still wasn't sure this was God, so I prayed, "Father, is this the answer? Am I not supposed to get a loan?" And did you know that I just felt a peace about it? So, then I walked back to the house and started figuring things out.

By this time, I think we had saved $30,000, and at the rate we were saving money, I would have been over 120 years old when we had enough money. I thought, *God, if this isn't You, I'm dead in the water*. So, I spent the next two weeks praying about all of this. I wanted to make sure that I was hearing from God. I did not want to go to tell my partners I was going to do this debt-free and then break my word. The Bible says that a godly man swears to his own hurt and changes not (Ps. 15:4). One thing I knew is that the more I prayed in tongues about it, the more I'd either feel peace or that peace would diminish.

So, after two weeks, I came to the manager of our ministry at the time and told him, "We are going to do this debt-free. If they come to me tomorrow with all of the $3.2 million that I needed, I'm not taking it." Sure enough, the very next day, another bank that we had also sought a loan through came and said, "We're going to approve you for $4 million."

I told them, "You missed it. It's too late," and turned it down. And in fourteen months, we had the $3.2 million, and we did it all debt-free! All of that came from praying in tongues and asking God for an interpretation. It was awesome!

I tell you, we have such a powerful gift! Jesus said he wasn't going to leave us without comfort (John 14:18). He left us the Holy Spirit, and He is more than enough for any problem that we have. Anything that we need, the Holy Spirit is not even challenged by these things.

Our ministry has grown tremendously since then, and now—as of this writing—we're believing God for $1 billion above our normal operating expenses, which at this time is about $7 million per month. You might be thinking, *A billion dollars is a lot!* But I remember when we were believing God for that $3.2 million. I didn't have it then, and yet through praying in tongues and interpreting, God showed me how He was going to provide. The Holy Spirit looks at $1 billion, and that's nothing to Him.

That's how God looks at whatever you're facing right now. It doesn't matter if it's a need in your body, finances, your marriage, or something else. If you will build yourself up on your most holy faith and edify yourself by speaking in tongues (Jude 20 and 1 Cor. 14:4) and then interpret (1 Cor. 14:13), He will give you the knowledge and wisdom to receive whatever it is that you need. This is how it works! Are you using these gifts that God has made available to you?

A Friend Came to Mind

One of the ways I keep my mind focused on the Lord when I pray in tongues is I will also pray with my understanding (1 Cor. 14:15). One day, I had been praying in tongues for maybe two hours, and an old friend came to mind. We used to attend the same Baptist church, but we had lost touch. I hadn't seen him in years. So, I spent the next thirty minutes to an hour praying for him, wondering about what's happening with him. Then the doorbell rang. I went to the door, and standing there was my old friend! He didn't even say hi; he just pushed me aside, walked in, sat down, and started crying.

> Are you using these gifts that God has made available to you?

He began pouring out his heart and telling me all of his problems. My first thought was, *Oh, man, I've been praying in tongues for two or three hours, and I could've been doing something that would've helped me minister to him.* Then my next thought was, *How would I have known that he was even going to come here?* All of a sudden, it dawned on me that I had been praying in tongues for him! That was the reason he came to mind! So, I just stopped him mid-sentence and started ministering to him through a word of knowledge and told him what to do.

Now, the last time this friend had seen me, I was a Baptist. We didn't believe in the baptism of the Holy Spirit. So, when I started operating in the gifts, it scared the liver out of him! He didn't know what was going on. But he knew that what I was saying was from the Lord, and he got set free. This is when I began to recognize the power of praying in tongues, that God would use it to reveal things to me.

I've also learned that you don't have to interpret what you're saying right at that moment. The reason is, you may have something come up the next day or the next week when you really need to hear that supernatural instruction. If God were to tell you everything your spirit was saying right after you prayed in tongues, it wouldn't apply. But when a situation comes up, you will just know what to do. This is what will happen when *you* pray in tongues too. You don't have to stop and immediately give an interpretation; you just need to have your understanding become fruitful (1 Cor. 14:13–14), which God will do at the right time.

I tell you, I pray in tongues a lot. I'll go walking an hour or two, and I usually spend an hour or more speaking in tongues and praying for an interpretation. Very little of what God has accomplished in my life is separate from this. You might not have realized that I speak in tongues, but if I hadn't received the baptism of the Holy Spirit, I wouldn't be where I am today. God has done awesome things in my life, and it all can be traced back to that.

SUPERNATURAL INTERVENTION AND BREAKTHROUGH

The final illustration I want to share with you is about a man who put his house on the market and asked God to sell it. But after two years, it hadn't sold. Finally, he heard me on television teaching about praying in tongues. So, he started operating in this gift. In two days' time, his house sold! A buyer came to him at closing and said, "Did you know that the very first day you put your house on the market, I told my wife, 'That's our house.' But for two years, I couldn't get the financing to buy your house. Then the strangest thing happened: Two days ago, somebody just came to me with cash to buy my house. That enabled me to close and then come and buy your house."

Now, see, there's no way in the natural that this could have happened without a supernatural intervention and breakthrough. This man sharing his testimony said he couldn't have known that his buyer was waiting for the finances to buy his own house. There were just limitations in the natural—variables that could only be resolved when he prayed in tongues. The Holy Spirit could make intercession through him (Rom. 8:26), and the whole thing worked out in short order. I'm telling you, this is the power that is available to you. You need to use it!

What I have shared with you is just a glimpse of the benefits of the baptism of the Holy Spirit. The enemy fights against the baptism of the Holy Spirit and speaking in tongues at best, to make this optional and, at worst, reject it as demonic. But if you can get a hold of what I'm saying, I guarantee your ability to hear God will increase. If you haven't received the baptism of the Holy Spirit, you need this gift. It will change your life!

If you've already been baptized in the Holy Spirit but you don't speak in tongues very often, you need to make a change. You have to deliberately, on purpose, exercise yourself in these gifts of speaking in tongues and asking for an interpretation. If you'll stop limiting the ways God can speak to you, you'll start receiving revelation for every area of your life!

CONCLUSION

I want to challenge you to begin to seek the Lord in hearing His voice in the four ways I have shared with you in this booklet. As I started off saying, God is always speaking. You just have to recognize His voice and tune in to the ways that He is speaking. Recognize that God is using your conscience to draw you to Himself. Don't ignore or violate this intuitive knowledge of right and wrong. It's foundational. Then go to the Word of God. It's anointed, and God will speak to you through the Scriptures. You just can't go very far if you don't know what the Word says. However, even though the Word is absolutely essential, it is not enough. If you're born again, you are one spirit with the Lord (1 Cor. 16:17), and He will speak to you Spirit to spirit. He will lead you by the peace of God acting as an umpire in your heart (Col. 3:15). You just need to delight in the Lord and put Him first. He will lead you by your desires.

Finally, as I just covered in the last chapter, another important way God speaks to through your spirit is through the baptism of the Holy Spirit, which comes with speaking in tongues. It's a powerful gift that, when coupled with interpretation of tongues, will give you supernatural revelation that you otherwise wouldn't have. It's how the apostle Paul received his revelation. If you don't have the baptism of the Holy Spirit, it's like charging hell with a water pistol! You need power (Acts 1:8).

I promise you that if you start operating in what I've shared with you, your ability to hear God's voice will go through the roof! You will get beyond just the physical, natural realm. Supernatural things will begin to happen around you, and in the lives of people you encounter.

There's a reason that some people hear God and others don't. The Holy Spirit is vital to this process, and you must allow Him to flow through you. My prayer is that you have been stirred up to go after what is available to you. You're not waiting on God; He is waiting on you. If you will draw near to Him, He will draw near to you (James 4:8). You will be hearing Him speak to you. I guarantee it!

FURTHER STUDY

If you enjoyed this booklet and would like to learn more about some of the things I've shared, I suggest my other teachings:

- *My Appointment with God*
- *Biblical Worldview: Foundational Truths*
- *Plain as Dirt*
- *Effortless Change*
- *How to Hear God's Voice*
- *10 Reasons It's Better to Have the Holy Spirit*
- *The New You and the Holy Spirit*

These teachings are available either free of charge at **awmi.net/video** or for purchase in book, study guide, CD, DVD, or USB formats at **awmi.net/store**.

RECEIVE JESUS AS YOUR SAVIOR

Choosing to receive Jesus Christ as your Lord and Savior is the most important decision you'll ever make!

God's Word promises, *"That if thou shalt confess with thy mouth the Lord Jesus, and shalt believe in thine heart that God hath raised him from the dead, thou shalt be saved. For with the heart man believeth unto righteousness; and with the mouth confession is made unto salvation"* (Rom. 10:9–10). *"For whosoever shall call upon the name of the Lord shall be saved"* (Rom. 10:13). By His grace, God has already done everything to provide salvation. Your part is simply to believe and receive.

Pray out loud: "Jesus, I acknowledge that I've sinned and need to receive what you did for the forgiveness of my sins. I confess that You are my Lord and Savior. I believe in my heart that God raised You from the dead. By faith in Your

Word, I receive salvation now. Thank You for saving me."

The very moment you commit your life to Jesus Christ, the truth of His Word instantly comes to pass in your spirit. Now that you're born again, there's a brand-new you!

Please contact us and let us know that you've prayed to receive Jesus as your Savior. We'd like to send you some free materials to help you on your new journey. Call our Helpline: **719-635-1111** (available 24 hours a day, seven days a week) to speak to a staff member who is here to help you understand and grow in your new relationship with the Lord.

Welcome to your new life!

RECEIVE
THE HOLY SPIRIT

A s His child, your loving heavenly Father wants to give you the supernatural power you need to live a new life. *"For every one that asketh receiveth; and he that seeketh findeth; and to him that knocketh it shall be opened…how much more shall your heavenly Father give the Holy Spirit to them that ask him?"* (Luke 11:10–13).

All you have to do is ask, believe, and receive!

Pray this: "Father, I recognize my need for Your power to live a new life. Please fill me with Your Holy Spirit. By faith, I receive it right now. Thank You for baptizing me. Holy Spirit, You are welcome in my life."

Some syllables from a language you don't recognize will rise up from your heart to your mouth (1 Cor. 14:14). As you speak them out loud by faith, you're releasing God's power from within and building yourself up in the spirit (1 Cor. 14:4). You can do this whenever and wherever you like.

It doesn't really matter whether you felt anything or not when you prayed to receive the Lord and His Spirit. If you believed in your heart that you received, then God's Word promises you did. *"Therefore I say unto you, What things soever ye desire, when ye pray, believe that ye receive them, and ye shall have them"* (Mark 11:24). God always honors His Word—believe it!

We would like to rejoice with you, pray with you, and answer any questions to help you understand more fully what has taken place in your life!

Please contact us to let us know that you've prayed to be filled with the Holy Spirit and to request the book *The New You & the Holy Spirit*. This book will explain in more detail about the benefits of being filled with the Holy Spirit and speaking in tongues. Call our Helpline: **719-635-1111** (available 24 hours a day, seven days a week).

CALL FOR PRAYER

If you need prayer for any reason, you can call our Helpline, 24 hours a day, seven days a week at **719-635-1111**. A trained prayer minister will answer your call and pray with you.

Every day, we receive testimonies of healings and other miracles from our Helpline, and we are ministering God's nearly-too-good-to-be-true message of the Gospel to more people than ever. So, I encourage you to call today!

About the Author

Andrew Wommack's life was forever changed the moment he encountered the supernatural love of God on March 23, 1968. As a renowned Bible teacher and author, Andrew has made it his mission to change the way the world sees God.

Andrew's vision is to go as far and deep with the Gospel as possible. His message goes far through the *Gospel Truth* television program, which is available to over half the world's population. The message goes deep through discipleship at Charis Bible College, headquartered in Woodland Park, Colorado. Founded in 1994, Charis has campuses across the United States and around the globe.

Andrew also has an extensive library of teaching materials in print, audio, and video. More than 200,000 hours of free teachings can be accessed at **awmi.net**.

CONTACT INFORMATION

Andrew Wommack Ministries, Inc.

PO Box 3333
Colorado Springs, CO 80934-3333
info@awmi.net
awmi.net

Helpline: 719-635-1111 (available 24/7)

Charis Bible College

info@charisbiblecollege.org
844-360-9577
CharisBibleCollege.org

For a complete list of all of our offices,
visit **awmi.net/contact-us**.

Connect with us on social media.